Original title:
A Window Full of Life

Copyright © 2025 Creative Arts Management OÜ
All rights reserved.

Author: Ophelia Ravenscroft
ISBN HARDBACK: 978-1-80581-800-7
ISBN PAPERBACK: 978-1-80581-327-9
ISBN EBOOK: 978-1-80581-800-7

Illuminated Frames of Memory

In a frame that's dusty and old,
Silly stories begin to unfold.
Cats in hats and dogs that sing,
Laughter echoes in this wild fling.

The couch holds secrets, snacks galore,
While socks are hiding behind the door.
Each glance reveals a tale untold,
Nutsy antics in frames of gold.

Soft Murmurs from the Outside

Birds gossip like friends at a cafe,
Chirps and tweets brighten the day.
Squirrels plot in the trees above,
Chasing shadows, they jump and shove.

A dog barks loud, with a comical twist,
As postmen pass, he can't be missed.
Laughter erupts, oh what a sight,
Joy spills out, morning feels just right.

The Dance of Leaves and Light

Leaves waltz on breezes that tease,
Dancing wildly, oh what a breeze!
Sunbeams tickle the squirrels' tails,
As they weave through the grassy trails.

A butterfly flutters, bold and bright,
While ants march on, with all their might.
Nature's stage is a comical show,
Full of mischief, it's the star of the flow.

Moments Caught in Sunlight

Sunlight spills like a pitcher poured,
Dust motes dance, the room's adored.
A cat prances, tail held high,
Pretending to be the king on high.

Children giggle with ice cream dreams,
Melting treats and funny schemes.
Each bite leads to sticky delight,
Caught in sunshine, life feels just right.

Light Streaming Through

Bright rays sneak in,
Like giggles in a room.
They tickle the curtains,
Chasing away the gloom.

Dust motes dance around,
Like tiny little stars.
They swirl and twist about,
In their whimsical cars.

A shadow spins and leaps,
Trying to steal the scene.
It trips on its own feet,
Then laughs as if it's keen.

Light bursts like popcorn,
Catch it quick, don't let go!
It bounces off the walls,
With a zippy-zappy glow.

Colors of Life's Canvas

A smear of yellow laughs,
With a wink of gleeful green.
Blue swirls up with glee,
As it joins the happy scene.

Red splashes have a chat,
With orange by its side.
They tell the best of jokes,
With no need to hide.

Purple's all dramatic,
Throwing fits, oh so loud!
While pink's just giggling,
Feeling pretty and proud.

Together they create,
A masterpiece so bright.
With crayons of laughter,
Painting joy day and night.

The View from Within

Inside these four small walls,
The antics never cease.
My cat pretends to pounce,
Giving us a comic feast.

The dog chases shadows,
With a thunderous create.
While kids build castles high,
Filling the floor with great fate.

Naps turn into battles,
When pillows start to fly.
Every corner bursts with giggles,
As we all duck and sigh.

From this lively lens,
The world seems quite absurd.
With laughter echoing loud,
Who needs to say a word?

Nature's Stained Canvas

There's paint upon the leaves,
Like splattered silly schemes.
The grass has sprouted jokes,
In vivid, wild dreams.

Squirrels in full costume,
Dressed up in fuzzy coats.
Playing hide and seek,
Making mischief with their notes.

The flowers all are gossiping,
With colors loud and bright.
They whisper 'bout the bees,
Who buzz about with delight.

Nature throws a party,
With colors in full swing.
Join in with the laughter,
And see what joy can bring.

Worlds Beyond Glass

In a frame where birds trot,
Squirrels plot their next big heist.
A cat, with eyes all aglow,
Wonders if it's a bird or roast.

Beyond the sill, a dog barks loud,
Chasing dreams on clouds of fur.
Meanwhile, my coffee cools down fast,
With laughter, I just chuckle and stir.

Reflections of Tomorrow

Outside, kids race on tiny bikes,
While I glare at my slowwork stack.
Tomorrow's plans whirl and twirl,
    But today? I'll just relax!

A bird lands and seems to mock,
With a dance that wobbles my mind.
I wonder if it's laughing too,
At this farce we call mankind.

Glimpses of Existence

Neighbors argue about their hedge,
While I munch my snacks with glee.
A squirrel steals my sandwich crumbs,
    And grins at the life that's free.

The sun dips low, it's starting to glow,
    A toddler's giggles rise above.
With every look outside I take,
I find more reason to laugh and love.

Framed Moments of Joy

Rain falls lightly, taps the pane,
To puddle-jumpers, it's a thrill.
But from my couch, I catch the show,
And gladly miss that slippery spill.

Through here, the world is full of quirks,
Each passerby a sitcom star.
I smile wide and sip my tea,
As everyday feels bizarre and far.

Whispers of the Outside

A squirrel dons shades, ready to play,
While pigeons gossip about their café.
The flowers dance funny in the breeze,
Each bloom a joker, aiming to please.

A cat in a hat observes from afar,
Juggling its toys like a circus star.
The sun winks down, a playful tease,
As the world spins round with giggles and ease.

The Liveliness Beyond

Kids on scooters race by with glee,
While ants march like soldiers, busy as can be.
A dog dons a cape, ready to fly,
Chasing its tail, oh what a sight, oh my!

Birds in a choir sing silly tunes,
As squirrels break dance under the moon.
Every moment outside is a blast,
With laughter and joy, life goes by fast.

A Portal to Vibrance

A butterfly tries to steal the show,
With polka-dot wings, it steals the glow.
A gopher pops up like a jack in the box,
Waving hello in mismatched socks!

The sun paints the scene with splashes so bright,
As insects perform their little ballet flight.
A cow plays harmonica, what a delight,
In this carnival scene, day turns to night.

The Glass Viewfinder

Lemons debate who's the zestiest slice,
While cucumbers giggle, oh isn't that nice?
A hedgehog in boots does the cha-cha-cha,
Whistling a tune, ta-da, ta-da!

Sunshine tickles each thing in its path,
As raindrops laugh, creating a bath.
Here's to the antics displayed outside,
In this humor-filled realm, let joy be the guide!

The Artistic Whisper of Seasons

Spring dances past, with a flowered hat,
While summer's charm rides a chubby cat.
Autumn's giggles toss leaves in the air,
As winter paints scenes of frosty despair.

Each season a trickster, in playful attire,
Juggling warm sunshine, and sparks of fire.
The clouds drop confetti, the stars wear a grin,
Nature's a circus, and we're all in!

Lively Reflections

In reflections of puddles, two frogs take a dive,
Racing each other, feeling alive.
They leap over ripples, with joy uncontained,
While a fish looks on, utterly entertained.

A squirrel in sunglasses, munching his snack,
Writes a memoir of the nuts he'll hack.
Each glance at the surface, reveals a new show,
And life's just a mirror where silliness flows!

The Buzz Beyond the Glass

Bees in their meetings buzz gossip so loud,
While butterflies strut like they're part of a crowd.
The ants hold a parade, with tiny drumsticks,
Marching in formation, their own little tricks.

Outside the pane, there's a dance with no end,
Where nature's odd characters always contend.
Laughter erupts from the blooms in a row,
As life through the glass puts on a grand show!

Ceaseless Wanderings

A raccoon in rain boots explores the yard,
With a map made of lettuce, he thinks it's not hard.
He stumbles on treasures, a spoon and a sock,
Laughing at mischief from a well-timed clock.

The wind howls at stories, whispered by trees,
Of glimpses and giggles, carried in leaves.
As clouds take a detour, and shadows are drawn,
Life skips like a pebble, from dusk until dawn!

A Story Told in Bloom

In the garden, blooms collide,
Daisies chatting, side by side.
Bees are buzzing with a grin,
Tickled by the pollen's spin.

Worms in soil, they wiggle free,
Wiggling tales of a wild spree.
Sunflowers strut with heads held high,
As butterflies dance low and shy.

Ladybugs play hide and seek,
With petals flirting, chic and sleek.
A rabbit hops, a squirrel prances,
While roses show off their best stances.

In this patch, laughter blooms bright,
Even the weeds join in the flight.
Nature's party, take a peek,
Where joy sneezes and flowers speak!

Fragments of Liveliness

The sun peeks in, a teasing ray,
Lighting up the chaos play.
A cat winks at a jester bug,
While ants dance a silly rug.

Laughter spills from a flower pot,
Garden gnomes are losing the plot.
Hummingbirds compete in flight,
Zooming past with sheer delight.

Tulips wear shades, looking cool,
Telling stories, bending the rule.
The veggies gossip in a line,
Radishes are laughing, feeling fine.

While clouds drift lazily above,
The raindrops fall, a gentle shove.
Together they share a silly cheer,
Fragments of life that we hold dear!

Echoes of Laughter and Light

Morning light skips on the grass,
Chasing shadows that try to pass.
Chirping birds in a feathery choir,
Singing songs that never tire.

A squirrel giggles, stealing a nut,
While daisies aim to take a cut.
The breeze hums a merry tune,
While butterflies swoop around in June.

Lemonade stands with sprightly kids,
Their laughter rolls like happy bids.
Sunbeams tickle the dragonflies,
As dragonflies soar through blue skies.

Echoes dance around the trees,
Whispering secrets on the breeze.
In this world, where joy swirls bright,
Laughter wraps us, pure delight!

Sunlit Stories

Under the sun, tales unfold,
Each petal whispers, brave and bold.
Frogs in ponds leap with a crack,
Towards butterflies painting the track.

Chubby bumblebees hum a song,
Buzzing where the flowers belong.
The sunflowers chuckle in rows,
While playing peek-a-boo with crows.

A ladybug twirls, red on green,
In this circus, laughter is seen.
Raindrops giggle, falling low,
Dancing 'til the big winds blow.

Sunlit stories weave through air,
With a tickle here, a playful flare.
Nature's canvas, forever bright,
Tusks of humor in pure delight!

Shades of Nature's Whimsy

Tiny birds in a dance,
Chatter and chirp at a glance.
Squirrels hop with glee,
As they plot their next spree.

Sunflowers wear silly hats,
Bouncing with cheer, like acrobats.
Butterflies join the cheer,
Fluttering in without fear.

A kitten peeks through the glass,
Wondering if all the fun will pass.
It paws at the air with flair,
Excited by the chaos out there.

A breeze steals away a shoe,
The shoes they have make quite the crew.
Nature's party can't be tamed,
In this life, we're all just named.

The Vibrant Abode

Look at the garden, so bright,
Gnomes wearing shades in delight.
Worms wiggle under the sun,
Making mud pies, oh what fun!

A frog leaps, a real show-off,
Sings his croak and lets out a scoff.
Ladybugs strut their stuff,
In a dress that's never too tough.

Trees gossip with leaves in a rustle,
While a cat tries not to tussle.
A squirrel with acorns aplenty,
Wants to share—his heart is empty.

Lizards sunbathe on the fence,
Striking poses without pretense.
Every day's a new charade,
In this lively escapade.

Stories Beyond the Pane

Peeking through the glass, oh dear,
A raccoon is stealing a beer!
While squirrels throw acorn snacks,
There's quite the ruckus at the backs.

The sun sets, colors jump and play,
As the dog chases shadows away.
Birds narrate their feathered tales,
With dramatic dips and wild trails.

A hedgehog rolls like a ball,
In the yard, he's having a ball.
The cats try to steal the scene,
Playing kings and queens, oh so keen.

With each glance at the world outside,
Laughter bubbles, we cannot hide.
These stories bubble, flash, and blend,
Life's an adventure with no end.

Kaleidoscope of Happenings

Rainbows splash after the rain,
Dancing colors, wild in the lane.
A snail races a lively bee,
On this path of whimsy we see.

Cows mooo with a rhythm divine,
Their hairy choir makes dinner fine.
Chickens strut like they own the place,
With feathers out, they win the race.

Clouds wear shades, drifting along,
While a kite tangled in a song.
The world spins in a colorful waltz,
Every misstep is someone's fault!

Glances through the glass reveal,
Life bursting at each little wheel.
In this kaleidoscope of glee,
It's hard to imagine we're not free!

The Colorful Gaze

Bees buzzing close, chasing a drip,
A squirrel in a tie takes a circus trip.
Down goes the flower, with a comedic frown,
While ants hold a party, they're the talk of the town.

A sunbeam dances, so bright on the floor,
A cat doing yoga, what's it stretching for?
A rainbow of colors, the day breaks out,
As the curtains flutter, the sun starts to shout.

Bouncing balloons caught on the sill,
The pigeons all gossip, what a wild thrill.
A frog leaps in, wearing a tiny hat,
Life's a big sketch that is drawn just like that.

Giggles outside as the children all play,
An old dog rolls over, he's lost in the fray.
Life is quite silly, let the laughter expand,
In this vibrant view, joy rides hand in hand.

Nature's Embrace in the Quiet

A snail in the garden thinks it's a fast lane,
While mushrooms look on, sporting little canes.
The breeze tells a joke that makes daisies cheer,
As a butterfly twirls, sipping nectar beer.

Grasshoppers giggle at a worm's silly dance,
While tree branches chuckle, giving nature a chance.
A robin wearing glasses reads a thick book,
While flowers gossip, on what kind of hook.

A hedgehog stumbles, it's all a big show,
In the quietest moments, wild laughter will grow.
Bees wear their headphones, lost in a tune,
While daisies have dreams of being the moon.

Nature's a comedian with jokes on replay,
In the heart of the garden, the wild things will stay.
Each laugh blooms brighter under the sun's glow,
In a world full of wonder, let the giggles flow.

The Portrait of an Afternoon

The sun paints the walls with splashes of cheer,
While shadows play tag, causing giggles to steer.
Two squirrels in suits are discussing their plans,
Creating a ruckus, while plotting their pranks.

A lazy old cat lounges, with a wink and a purr,
Observing the chaos, like a fluffy curator.
With a flip of its tail, more mischief begins,
As sparrows all gather, to cheer on the wins.

The breeze plays a tune, with leaves in the air,
And crickets compose, quite a curious fare.
A dog catches dreams, though their value is low,
As butterflies flutter, with a humorous glow.

The day wraps in laughter, a soft, warm embrace,
This portrait of silliness, brings a smile to the face.
In the heart of the afternoon, let giggles ignite,
As nature's own canvas becomes a delight.

Visions through the Glass

Through the pane, life winks, with a cheeky grin,
As raindrops perform, with a tap and a spin.
A squirrel in sneakers jumps over a crack,
While pigeons debate on who's next for a snack.

The sun peeks and giggles, spreading rays of fun,
As flowers wear hats, having their own pun.
A wallflower whispers to a petunia bright,
"Why don't we join in? It's such a delight!"

A butterfly slides in, with a dance and a swish,
And a ladybug shouts, "What do you wish?"
Clouds roll like tumbleweeds, soft and so grand,
As the world plays outside, in a whimsical band.

Through the glass, bright scenes cast shadows that sway,
Where laughter erupts, guiding all in its play.
In visions of joy, through the pane we'll all see,
Life's quirky adventures dancing wild and free.

The Living Canvas

Colors splashed, a paintbrush fight,
Birds in bowties, what a sight!
Squirrels snicker, nuts in hand,
Painting chaos, isn't life grand?

Butterflies wearing hats so tall,
Ducks that dance and bunnies crawl.
Every splash, a giggle caught,
Who knew nature had such thought?

Canvas laughs, tickled by breeze,
Trees giggle while swaying at ease.
A laugh from the grass, a chuckle too,
Life's art show, always something new.

Breathing Scenes

The clouds play tag, what a game,
Raindrops giggle as they aim.
Trees are swaying with the beat,
Nature's concert, oh so sweet!

A deer in glasses, reading a book,
While rabbits jump and rooks all look.
Nature's whims, simple yet bright,
Every glance brings pure delight.

Frogs wear crowns, king of the pond,
With each splash, new joy is spawned.
Hares tap dance, waves in cheer,
Breathing scenes, happy to be near.

Nature's Spectacle in Fragments

Little snippets fill the frame,
Bees with mustaches, all the same.
Chickens chat in silly tones,
Mice playing chess with sticks and stones.

Sunsets wear their party hats,
While fireflies flirt, the nighttime chats.
Laughter echoes in the trees,
Nature's echoes bring us ease.

Puddles jump with splashes loud,
A cat with glasses looks so proud.
Fragments of joy, our hearts they tickle,
Life's a show, with every giggle.

Daydreams Against the Glass

Snowflakes twerk, the winter's song,
While squirrels strut, they won't be long.
The sun can't help but wink and glare,
As shadows play with no real care.

Lizards laugh, basking in light,
While ants march on with all their might.
Daydreams swirl in frames so bright,
Who knew nature's tales took flight?

The moon's a jester in the night,
Wearing stars, oh what a sight!
Every glance at the glass brings cheer,
In this playful world, everything's clear.

The Living Collage

Framed in wood, where chaos reigns,
Cats chase dust while muffins gain.
Balloons float high, through puddles they dance,
A parrot squawks, it's got no chance.

Little kids draw on the wall,
One says, "Look! I made a stall!"
Ice cream melts on a sunny day,
Just enough for ants to play.

The goldfish glares, like it's the boss,
While that old plant thinks it's a gloss.
Each scratch and scribble tells a tale,
Of laughing faces, every detail.

Jelly spills on the floor so bright,
A sticky mess, but what a sight!
Laughter echoes through the rooms,
In this collage, joy resumes.

Melodies of the Unseen

Underneath the glowing moon,
A raccoon dances to a tune.
Socks are mismatched, a sight so grand,
As birdies chirp in sweet command.

A squirrel's got a secret stash,
Of glitter pens and candy trash.
Each note a giggle, each laugh a cheer,
Tickling the ears of all those near.

Invisible music fills the air,
Whispers of joy without a care.
The bee hums low, the breeze hums high,
In melodies, the spirits fly.

Pie fights break into a song,
While spaghetti's splattered all along.
In this concert, silly and free,
Life's a melody, just wait and see.

A Chronicle of Light

Sunbeams peek through dusty blinds,
Dancing shadows, what fun it finds.
A dogdreams loud, it snoozes and wriggles,
While its owner giggles and jiggles.

Pancakes flip with a sassy flair,
Syrup drips down without a care.
Each golden layer tells a tale,
Of mornings bright that never pale.

The clock ticks funny, it spins around,
Strange conversations, such silly sound.
The light ignites the smiles we share,
In this chronicle, love is everywhere.

Under rainbows or sunny light,
Every glance is a silly sight.
In this journal, laughter is bright,
With every moment, pure delight.

Whirling Skies and Dreaming Hearts

Kites that swirl in breezy climes,
Catch the laughter, bells, and chimes.
A child spins fast, a dizzy whirl,
Their giggles burst, like colors' swirl.

Clouds are fluff, like candy dreams,
Tickling noses, or so it seems.
In the gentlest breeze, worries untie,
As butterflies flutter and butterflies fly.

Out in the fields, a picnic won,
Sandwiches fight for the last crumb.
Each smile a spark in the skies so bright,
With dreaming hearts that soar in flight.

In this chaos, joy rejoices,
Echoing laughter fills the choices.
With whirling skies, a playful chart,
Together we craft, where love imparts.

Life's Tapestry Unfurled

Through the glass, the cat jumps high,
Chasing birds that flutter by.
A moment's notice makes me chuckle,
As he lands with a goofy huddle.

Children play with their grand ideas,
Building castles made of cheers.
While dogs next door bark at the sky,
Thinking they can also fly.

Socks and shoes left on the lawn,
Worn as trophies since the dawn.
Neighbors smile, a wave or two,
Life's a circus, who knew?

Flowers dance with the gentle breeze,
Waving back with such great ease.
And from above, a pigeon prances,
Dropping—let's just say—unexpected chances.

The Vibrant Spectrum of Days

Each morning brings a wild surprise,
Like toast that always seems to rise.
My coffee spills, it leaves a trail,
Like a ship that's lost its sail.

Sunlight dips in a golden hue,
As ducks parade, they honk, 'What's new?'
My neighbor's hat flies off his head,
Oh look, it's dancing—better fled!

A squirrel steals from the bird's bowl,
Feathers fly, it's on a roll.
I laugh at nature's comic play,
Who knew breakfast could betray?

Day fades into a colorful snooze,
Fireflies flicker, sharing clues.
Life's a painting, yes it's true,
Each stroke's a giggle, just for you.

Chasing Shadows in Light

Shadows leap in playful fights,
Dancing on walls and ceiling heights.
With every tick of the clock's hand,
Rigging pranks, oh isn't it grand?

A cat plays tricks with a flicking tail,
As the dog plans an epic fail.
Lowly grumbles of a tired chair,
Who knew it could have such flair?

Office plants gossip in the shade,
"Did you see that prank he made?"
Meanwhile the sun takes its grand bow,
Filling the room—oh, wow!

Night falls and stars giggle bright,
Mocking the moon for its clumsy flight.
Life's a jest—it's all in fun,
In this circus, we've just begun!

A Portal to Everyday Wonders

Behind the glass, the world's alive,
With a dance that makes me thrive.
A ladybug struts with such great flair,
Showing off her polka dot wear.

Kids on scooters race with glee,
While ice cream melts into a spree.
A dog digs deep in a sunny mound,
Forget about lunch—he's treasure found!

Bubbles float, a whimsical show,
Popping laughter as they go.
The wind chimes sing a silly tune,
As the clock ticks by in playful swoon.

Each glance reveals a funny sight,
Life's filled with whimsy and delight.
So peek through your glass and see,
The juggling world is wild and free!

Beyond the Transparent Barrier

Behind glass, a cat loves to stare,
With squirrels and birds, it dreams in mid-air.
The dog next door thinks it owns the block,
While the parrot quips, 'You folks are a flock!'

As shadows dance and sunlight prances,
We tiptoe, trapping our silly glances.
A raccoon sneaks past with a plan discreet,
Prompting the owl to admit defeat.

The world outside is a sitcom gone wild,
Each creature, a character, fanged and mild.
The goldfish laughs as it wiggles in glee,
Saying, 'Hey you, come enjoy the spree!'

So let's enjoy the ruckus and cheers,
Through the glass, we see life over the years.
With every flap, wiggle, and screech,
This quirky view, oh so fun to breach!

A Panoply of Colors

Sunflowers dance in a rainbow parade,
While the tomatoes play hide and evade.
The bees hum a tune to the butterflies' cheer,
As they gossip about the crops growing near.

Each hue splashes joy beyond the pane,
The oranges wink, teasing the grain.
The carrots converse with the radish crew,
'With this great harvest, what next shall we do?'

A peacock struts with a flamboyant flair,
While cabbages whisper, 'Do we even care?'
The corn stalks nod, all leafy and tall,
Saying aloud, 'Let's throw a grand ball!'

In this bizarre garden, we giggle and play,
As nature's madness unfolds every day.
With a burst of laughter, frills and fronds,
Life's vibrant palette continues to respond!

The World in a Bright Square

In the square, the pigeons plot and coo,
While the children chase shadows in a game or two.
An old man feeds them with crumbs and a grin,
Saying, 'Watch out for swoops, or you'll wear a pin!'

The ice cream truck chimes with a jingle and joy,
As kids giggle, chasing it like a toy.
The park bench holds tales of old and new,
While squirrels debate who has the best view.

A juggler performs with a wink and a laugh,
As dogs take their owners for a silly path.
The sunlight shimmers on this scene so bright,
Making every moment a delightful sight.

In our square, spontaneity is king,
Where laughter and chirps in harmony sing.
With every twist and turn, life starts to soar,
In this vibrant domain, there's always more!

Life's Celestial Gallery

Stars wink down from their lofty stage,
While clouds drift by, a fluffy, wild page.
The moon cracks jokes with a twinkling sound,
As night wraps the world, snug all around.

A comet zooms by, shouting, 'Hey, catch me!'
While fireflies dance in a buzzing spree.
The constellations whisper secrets of old,
Sharing tales of adventures and wonders untold.

Meteor showers sprinkle magic and play,
As families gather to gaze and to sway.
'Watch out,' says the owl, 'that's a shooting star!'
Wishing for snacks, and not just from afar.

In this gallery of celestial art,
Every twinkle, every flicker, shines from the heart.
Laughs and dreams woven into the night,
Creating a cosmos of pure delight!

The Palette of Perpetuity

Colors splashed on every pane,
Birds are singing, what a gain!
A squirrel dances with a twist,
Who knew the world could be such a tryst?

Sunlight spills, a golden hue,
Painting shadows, tried and true.
Butterflies flutter, make a fuss,
A game of tag with a passing bus.

Winking cats on sill so wide,
Napping dogs with love and pride.
They watch the antics, oh so grand,
Life's a circus, close at hand!

Peeking out, what do I see?
Neighbors arguing over tea.
Laughter echoes, joy is rife,
Oh, the chaos makes up life!

Frames of Serendipity

Frames depicting tales untold,
Like dogs in hats, so bold!
A parade of ducks on the street,
Who knew they'd breakdance on their feet?

Cactus plants don tiny coats,
As if they're prepping for a boat.
The sunflowers nod, quite the sight,
Each petal holding every delight.

Rain clouds wear a fuzzy cap,
As they gather for a nap.
Carrots jog, while onions cheer,
A veggie marathon, oh dear!

From my spot, it's plain to see,
Life's a joke, a comedy spree.
Each day a sketch, laughter flows,
In frames of joy, anything goes!

The Day's Transition

Morning light, a sleepy yawn,
Cats demand their classic spawn.
With coffee brewing, smells awake,
I wave at ducks learning to quake.

In the afternoons, bees perform,
Doing dances, quite the norm.
Umbrellas flip with sudden gusts,
Oh no! The bread got covered in rust!

As twilight falls, we see the show,
Fireflies twinkling in a row.
Laughter bubbles, stories bloom,
Kittens plotting till the gloom.

Night descends with whispers slight,
And dreams begin their nightly flight.
So grab a snack, sit down, and wait,
For tomorrow's silliness to create!

The Quiet Cascade of Life

Life flows gently, soft and nice,
As frogs go hopping, oh so precise.
Clouds stretch wide, like cozy beds,
While grass is home to many heads.

The wind chuckles through the leaves,
Rustling tales that nature weaves.
A lazy cat thinks it's all grand,
While worms dance thick in the sand.

Afternoon brings silly sights,
Gnomes in gardens having fights.
With pizza pies and hula hoops,
The world's a party, full of loops!

Moonlight spills on sleepy charms,
Every critter hugs their arms.
With chirps and grunts, dreams take flight,
In the cascade of laughter tonight!

Intricate Patterns of Beauty

Through glassy panes the world unfolds,
Colors dance in stories told.
Insects buzzing, birds at play,
Nature's jesters, all display.

Socks upon the clothesline sway,
As neighbors gossip, come what may.
Cats in sunbeams dozing deep,
Off on adventures, they rarely leap.

Outside, a child trips and falls,
Laughter echoes past the walls.
Ice cream drips onto the street,
Sticky fingers, life's little treat.

A squirrel scampers, steals a prize,
Acorns gathered, oh, so wise.
The sun sets low, a golden hue,
Life's a circus, and we're the crew.

A Scene Unfolded

Peeking out, I spy a pup,
Chasing shadows, eyes all up.
His tail a flag, his tongue a kite,
Bounding dreams in morning light.

Garden gnomes stand stiff and mute,
As kids proclaim, "Let's loot the loot!"
With treasures of the backyard kind,
Marbles, rocks, and ribbons twined.

Muffled giggles, whispers blend,
As friends create a secret trend.
A paper boat, a daring sail,
With every splash, they laugh and pale.

Across the street, a grumpy man,
Arguing with a passing van.
Yet through the chaos, joy remains,
Life's a wacky, wild campaign.

Symphony in the Frame

Through the glass, the world plays tunes,
With honking horns and bouncing balloons.
A toddler squeals in pure delight,
While dogs and cats engage in fights.

Barking at postmen, running fast,
This tiny drama, a glorious cast.
Birds chirp symphonies from the trees,
Nature's melodies float with ease.

A cloud rolls by, a pirate's hat,
While ants march by, a tiny chat.
The sun peeks in, a cheeky grin,
As life's odd rhythms swirl within.

A lizard lounges, sunbaked still,
Chasing sunlight, a playful thrill.
Moments captured, laughter shared,
In this grand show, we're all ensnared.

Tumbling Raindrops and Radiant Sun

Raindrops tumble, tap-dance loud,
On rooftops singing, oh so proud.
Puddles form a wobbly stage,
Kids leap in, releasing rage.

Umbrellas flip in playful shame,
As laughter echoes, what a game!
Splashing waters, soaked to the skin,
A water fight, let the fun begin!

Sunlight breaks through clouds so gray,
Painting rainbows where shadows lay.
The park transforms, a bright parade,
With rubber ducks that never fade.

As dusk approaches, squeals still ring,
From little joys that summer bring.
With each drop, a tale unspun,
In playful chaos, we all run.

The Threshold of Sight

In the day, the cat perches proud,
Observing the world, unbowed.
Birds scatter, while squirrels play,
Her royal watch is the highlight of the day.

Neighbours walk their dogs in glee,
One trips over, laughter for free.
The antics unfold, a grand parade,
Who knew such joy could be made!

A flower pot tips, down it goes,
The dog thinks it's a game, who knows?
Life's a comedy, a scripted flair,
With each little mishap, I can only stare.

As the sun sets, shadows grow tall,
The tales of the day, I've seen it all.
From a spot by the sill, my throne of delight,
Every little moment, a reason to write.

Windowsill Chronicles

A bumblebee buzzes, a clown in disguise,
Flitting around, oh what a surprise!
It tumbles and plops, but gets up with pride,
In this microcosm, what fun do we find?

The neighbor's duck waddles, a pompous strut,
Cracking the code of an open nut.
With quacks and a splash, in the puddle it dives,
Life's unexpected joys, it always survives!

Ants form a line, with pies made of crumbs,
Marching along, a band of tiny drums.
A leaf falls soft, right on my tea,
Who knew nature's chaos would be so funny?

As dusk drapes in with a pink-purple hue,
The sill becomes host to a roosting blue parrot too.
Reflecting on all, beneath the moon's gleam,
Every frolicking moment, life's zany dream!

A Glimpse into Eden

From the ledge, I spy all the fun,
A squirrel singing, thinking he's the one.
He leaps and he bounds, a fur-coated star,
With a passion for acorns, he raises the bar.

A couple walks by, all lovey-dovey,
Until they trip over that same red puppy.
Laughter erupts, hearts in the sprint,
Together they giggle, finding love in a hint.

An owl hoots loudly, trying to be wise,
But misjudges a branch and tumbles to size.
Nature's great humor sprawled all around,
Each moment of gaffe, more smiles to compound.

The sunset blushes, what a silly display,
Echoes of laughter blending with the day.
Together we gather, a peculiar blend,
In this slice of chaos, life has no end.

Reflections of Joy

Through the glass, a world unfolds,
Socks mismatched, personalities bold.
Each passerby, a character new,
Collecting stories, oh if they only knew!

A cat with a hat peeks out to play,
While the dog next door chases his own tail away.
The laughter cascades, from window to street,
Life's little quirks make a treat so sweet.

Kids on their bikes, zigzagging by,
One flies off curb, dreams touch the sky.
Parents gasp, but laughter won the day,
Their love is the glue that holds all at bay.

As night falls gentle and twinkling stars gleam,
Reflections of joy dance in the moonbeam.
From this little perch, I watch and I sigh,
Life is a punchline—oh me, oh my!

Horizons of Hope

In a house so full of cheer,
There's a parrot named Pierre.
He sings in rhyme, oh what a guy,
While the cat just rolls her eye.

Beneath the sun, a dog runs fast,
Chasing shadows, none will last.
The goldfish stares with big surprise,
As squirrels taunt him from the skies.

A child peeks through a frame so wide,
Imagining a giant slide.
The mailbox dances with a jig,
Dreaming of a sandwich big.

As rain comes down, in drops it plays,
Dancing knots like tiny rays.
Live life loud, grab a donut treat,
The world outside can't be beat!

The Dance of the Elements

The wind swirls leaves in crazy loops,
While the sun winks at all the scoops.
A cloud, with fluff and jokes to share,
Hiccups water in midair.

The trees are swaying to a beat,
Twirling root and barking feet.
A squirrel scolds the setting sun,
'You think you beat us? Not much fun!'

Raindrops tumble like tiny clowns,
Splashing puddles, joy abounds.
The rainbow whispers, 'Take a ride!
You might just find the other side!'

In this dance, every twist and turn,
Brings laughter, fun, and some concern.
So leap and bound, don't take a pause,
In nature's show, we find our cause!

Bright Narratives

Where colors play in a sunny glare,
Stories dance through warm, sweet air.
An ant in shades, a hat on tight,
Looks like he's going out tonight!

A bicycle with clownish bells,
Rides on by, where laughter swells.
The flowers giggle, petals sway,
As bugs all gather for ballet.

The moon peeks through a curtain seam,
Crafting tales from a dreamy stream.
A raccoon wearing pajamas bright,
Takes the stage for the night's delight.

Underneath the starlit dome,
Each laugh and story feels like home.
With every glance, a joy ignites,
Life's little quirks bring pure delights!

The Living Picture

Canvas alive with spark and cheer,
A paint splatter throws its spear.
A cat in blue, a dog in green,
Who knew art could be so keen?

A sandwich dances, jelly on top,
With lettuce and laughter, it won't stop.
Each slice wiggles, a merry groove,
While crumbs cascade in joyous move.

In the corner, a clock does spin,
Tick-tock, tick-tock, where to begin?
A turtle breaks into a trot,
Claiming 'Art is not just for thought!'

Filled with color, joy, and fun,
Life's a canvas for everyone.
With each brushstroke, a smile we find,
In this lively art, we are entwined!

Echoes of Laughter

In a room where giggles play,
The cat's the jester, on display.
He wears a hat, all crooked style,
Chasing his tail, oh what a mile!

Cookies crumble on the floor,
Knock-knock jokes slam the door.
An echo sails, like paper planes,
In this house, joy reigns like trains.

Friends gather, a silly crew,
Telling tales, both old and new.
With bites of pie and laughter loud,
We dance around, a merry crowd.

When shadows dance and daylight fades,
The tales grow wild in silly cascades.
Though mischief brews like morning dew,
In this place, there's always room for two.

Shadows and Sunlight

Sunlight pours with golden beams,
Where shadows stretch in playful schemes.
The dog's a shadow, chased by light,
Rolling in grass, what a delight!

Birds chirp tunes from tree-top highs,
While squirrels plot their grand reprise.
With every flutter, a giggle beams,
As nature's stage performs in dreams.

A moth alights on grandma's hat,
She swats it hard, and down it sat.
Laughter bubbles, fills the air,
In this theatre of love and care.

When shadows skulk and sunlight fades,
The world's a jest with silly blades.
In this garden, joy's in flight,
Silly moments shine so bright!

Breaths of Fresh Air

In the park, where breezes play,
Laughter floats, it leads the way.
Kids on swings, heads in the sky,
As kites loop up and races fly.

A picnic spread with crumbs galore,
The ants march in, we can't ignore!
A sandwich flies, oh what a feast,
When nature calls, we're all released.

There's grandpa dancing with a broom,
In this garden, no talk of gloom.
With every sneeze that brings a smile,
We take a breath, let joy compile.

So chase the clouds, let spirits soar,
In the fresh air, there's always more.
As laughter mingles with the breeze,
We find our peace, with such great ease.

The Open Frame

An open frame to view the day,
Hosts a show where sillies play.
Neighbors wave, and jokes collide,
Behind this frame, no need to hide.

Birds in hats and squirrels that sing,
Set the stage for everything.
As laughter rings and stories bloom,
Life's just a wacky, bright costume!

With every knock and every cheer,
Visitors come, their faces clear.
Through this glass, we spin our tales,
As joy rides high on crazy trails.

So let the world, in whimsy, thrive,
In this picture, we feel alive.
With snapshots made of laughter's light,
The frame is rich, our hearts take flight!

Verdant Tales Unseen

In a garden where gnomes conspire,
The daisies gossip, the weeds admire.
A snail rehearses a slow-baked play,
While ants debate on the best snacks of the day.

Petunias giggle in whispered hues,
As butterflies dance in their playful shoes.
A rabbit's wiggle, a hedgehog's sigh,
Life's a circus, beneath the sky!

The sun wears shades, taking a break,
While the moon laughs, making stars quake.
Clouds perform with a fluffy puff,
"Life's too funny, enough's enough!"

In this lush realm, mischief ignites,
Tickling the leaves, enjoying delights.
With every rustle and wave of a vine,
Nature chuckles, all is fine!

Glimpse of the Garden's Heart

A tomato talks with the old garden hose,
Sharing secrets no one else knows.
Bees wear hats made of buttercup gold,
While worms boast stories that never get old.

A sunflower yawns, stretching its rays,
While sprouts play hopscotch in sunny displays.
Dandelions giggle at shadows they cast,
While crickets chirp tunes that'll always last.

A frog in a tux, singing at noon,
Winks at the moon, sharing a tune.
The lettuce romances with soft summer breeze,
Life in the garden is sure to please.

Their chatter and laughter weave through the night,
Each twinkling star joins the jovial plight.
In this jolly patch, the magic is clear,
Nature's punchline brings everyone cheer!

The Veil of Seasons

Spring brings secrets on buds' little lips,
With bees in tuxedos and flower pet tips.
Budgies in bow ties, they lecture the blooms,
"Life's a party! Let's burst out in glooms!"

Summer's a jester with rays cheeky bright,
The grass tickles toes to start a good fight.
Watermelons laugh, splattering around,
While sunflowers spin in their merry surround.

Fall dresses up in a patchwork of fun,
Pumpkins tell tales 'til the day is done.
Squirrels play hide-and-seek with delight,
Gathering acorns 'til late in the night.

Winter arrives with its coat of white fluff,
But snowmen joke, saying, "This isn't so tough!"
The seasons are playing, a grand game of tags,
With giggles and wiggles and beautiful gags!

Fragments of Daydreams

Butterflies wear spectacles, reading the breeze,
As daisies spin tales of whimsical tease.
A ladybug plans a sky-high parade,
While the shadows join in, not to be swayed.

The wind writes poems in swirling delight,
Tickling the grass, holding daydreams tight.
Rabbits who tumble in patches of green,
Chase sunlight instead of chasing the scene.

In the hush of a garden, the fireflies blink,
While frogs on lily pads lean back to think.
Each leaf holds a secret, a laugh in disguise,
Nature's a jest, a splendid surprise.

As the sun bows low, waving goodnight,
The stars slip in, eager to unite.
With dreams all around, the garden will cheer,
For laughter and life are always right here!

Beyond the Pane

Sunlight dances, a playful sprite,
Cats on a sill, in their own delight.
Birds gossip loudly, making a fuss,
While squirrels plan heists, oh what a plus!

Rain taps a rhythm, a silly beat,
Pigeons parade, strutting their feet.
The neighbor's dog barks, he thinks he's cool,
When all he's got is a drool as a jewel.

A leaf flutters down, doing a twirl,
As children outside spin, jump and whirl.
Their laughter echoes, a sweet serenade,
While the world turns wild in this grand charade.

Time flies by, and with all its quirks,
The pane stays clear, as the fun just works.
What a view, so absurd and bright,
In this little frame, oh what a sight!

The View Beyond Stillness

Gazing afar, the world waves back,
Bees crash the scene with a clumsy attack.
Flowers gossip, in colors so loud,
As butterflies flaunt, feeling quite proud.

A dog in a tutu prances along,
While ants have a meeting, discussing who's strong.
Laughter erupts from pots on a shelf,
As the spoons start to dance, oh who needs help?

The clouds do a shuffle, a happy parade,
While raindrops compete for a splash on the jade.
Each moment a giggle, each tick a surprise,
Oh, the stories unfold right before our eyes.

Nature's a theater, with quirks to unwind,
Through panes of our lives, such joy we find.
Each glance outside, a comical spree,
In the cosmic comedy, so wild and free!

Glass Reflections of Nature

Through glass it's a mess, a raucous affair,
Where shadows play tricks, and light finds its flair.
A cat leaps, then slips, on a sunbeam's form,
Creating a spectacle, the norm's out of norm.

The wind whispers jokes as it tickles the trees,
While flowers crack puns riding on the breeze.
A squirrel poses, like he's the main act,
Inventing new stunts, and that's how they're packed.

Reflections of chaos, with glasses so clear,
Where mirth reigns supreme, simply drawing us near.
Butterflies giggle, tickling the air,
While the world spins around without a single care.

What joy lies within, all wrapped in a glow,
Nature's own antics, its whimsical show.
So raise up a toast, through this crystal divide,
To the laughter and life, what a joyful ride!

Scenes from the Heart

In my little corner, the world has a laugh,
With bright little critters, writing their own paragraph.
A turtle once fast, now takes it real slow,
As if pondering life, or just putting on a show.

The clouds roll by, making funny faces,
While the sun crinkles laughs in its warm embraces.
A flower sneezes, petals scatter with glee,
And the grass makes a joke, saying, 'Look at me!'

A child runs out, with giggles galore,
Chasing the wind like a playful folklore.
Mice play the banjo, and frogs clap along,
While shadows join in for a jubilant song.

Scenes from the heart, full of mirth and delight,
In this kaleidoscope, the colors are bright.
Let's cheer for the moments that make us all grin,
For life outside's a stage, where the fun can begin!

Echoes of Connectivity

Through the glass, I see my cat,
Chasing shadows, what is that?
A squirrel mocks with cheeky flair,
Nature's talk show, everywhere!

Birds tweet their gossip by my sill,
Peeking in, they've got the thrill.
Each fluttering wing lends a tale,
As I sip coffee, inhale, exhale!

The neighbor's dog joins in the fun,
Barking at everyone who runs.
With each glance, life's quirks unfold,
A comedy show, bright and bold!

So here I sit, a viewer blessed,
In this frame, I'm truly jested.
With laughter ringing, joy takes flight,
Outside my glass, it's pure delight!

Life's Abundant Canvas

Colors pop and swirl anew,
With each breeze, there's much to do.
A painter splashes joy and cheer,
In vibrant hues that reappear.

Kids run by with ice cream cones,
Dripping colors, sticky tones.
Laughter bounces off the walls,
Echoes where the sunshine calls.

Roses bloomed, a mischievous cat,
Knocks them down—oh, what of that?
Each petal falls, a cheeky wink,
Nature's art makes me think!

So I muse at the lively scene,
Of busy bees and greens that gleam.
In this sketch of daily grind,
Joy is the masterpiece we find!

Garden of Glimpses

Peeking out, I spy the fun,
My garden's buzzing like a gun.
Bees in bloom, they dance and twirl,
A wild party in the swirl!

Mr. Frog, his royal grace,
Takes a leap from place to place.
While ladybugs play hide and seek,
Life's chaos makes me giggle, peek!

The gnome, he stands with silly grin,
Watching chaos that's all within.
With every rustle, laughter grows,
In my tiny world, joy just flows!

So here I gaze, the grass is high,
A jester's stage beneath the sky.
Amidst the blooms, I find my cheer,
In this green space, life's jokes appear!

Framed Whispers of Existence

In the frame of my sunny seat,
Life's whispers gather, oh so sweet.
With the rustling leaves, they conspire,
Tales of antics, hopes, and fire.

A squirrel's acrobatics, oh my!
Flipping 'round, he leaps so high.
While ants march like little troops,
Their tiny feet dance in loops!

Wind chimes tinkle tunes so bright,
As birds chirp in the morning light.
Each sound a note in nature's song,
In this framed world, I feel I belong!

So watch the show from your own chair,
Life outside, oh, what a flare!
With a giggle, I raise my glass,
To the whims of life, let's raise a laugh!

The Border of Reality

Peeking through the glass so bright,
I see a cat that thinks it's a knight.
An army of ants in single file,
drama unfolds with every smile.

Squirrels in capes, they dart and dash,
while birds judge them with a splash.
A dog debates the fence with flair,
a world of giggles in the air.

A snail on a quest, slow and grand,
plotting to conquer the garden land.
Spring flowers bloom with gossip loud,
sharing secrets, oh so proud.

Reality bends, a fun-filled spree,
as I sip tea on my balcony.
The lines between normal and bizarre,
dissolve with laughter, sweet as a star.

The Quiet Symphony

In the stillness, a cricket plays,
his melody quirks in mysterious ways.
A squirrel spins tales of bold exploits,
as a chorus of frogs hums with hoots.

The wind sneaks in with a cheeky nudge,
as flowers bloom, and neighbors grudge.
A paper airplane takes flight with glee,
crashing on rooftops like it's meant to be.

A ladybug winks, red and round,
a stampede of raindrops hits the ground.
Sunshine giggles, tickling the scene,
while shadows dance like a dream machine.

So here we find, amidst the hum,
a symphony born from quiet fun.
Life's orchestra finds its groove and sway,
as laughter lingers through the day.

Life's Flickering Tapestry

Life stitches on with threads of gold,
a tale of small things never told.
A butterfly sneezes, takes to the air,
a whimsical dance with no care.

Mice in tuxedos waltz on the floor,
cracking jokes right by the door.
While the sun plays peek, a mischievous tease,
chasing shadows among the trees.

Bees join in, buzzing a tune,
as clouds drift by wearing hats like a boon.
A dog with a bowtie, eager to prance,
a sparkle of joy in every chance.

Life's a quilt, stitched with laughter,
each square a moment, a silly chapter.
Flickering bright, this tapestry gleams,
a funny parade of our wildest dreams.

Scenes of the Untold

Through the pane, a movie unfurls,
as ducks in capes do swirls and twirls.
The grass whispers secrets, 'Hey, look here!'
a mirthful scene, unabashed cheer.

The trees don hats, in posh display,
as clouds gossip and float away.
A raccoon, a thief, in the bin of snacks,
as laughter erupts from nature's tracks.

The sun, a comedian, tosses its rays,
with shadows that join in the joke-filled play.
A dance of laughter spills on the ground,
while whispers of joy are all around.

In this film of life, each laugh retold,
breaks norms and frames fine and bold.
A window to wild, a scene that molds,
a gallery of giggles, chaos unfolds.

Telling Tales in Bright Hues

Colors dance on walls so bright,
Silly shapes that twist in flight.
Laughter bubbles, splashes wide,
Joyful mischief can't abide.

A cat in socks, a dog with shades,
Chasing dreams in sunlit glades.
Every hue a tale to share,
With whimsy floating everywhere.

A fish that sings, a bird that jives,
In this place, imagination thrives.
Every glance a story spun,
Where laughter reigns and hugs are fun.

So paint your heart in colors bold,
Let every glance bring tales retold.
In this bright world, we take a dive,
Where even shadows seem alive.

A Veil of Vibrancy

A curtain sways, it giggles too,
Behind it hides a playful crew.
They peek and poke, a funny sight,
In the playful morning light.

A snail wears stripes, a worm in jazz,
Their laughter echoes, oh what a spazz!
Butterflies wear their fanciest flair,
Dancing on whispers, floating in air.

The sun spills soda, sweet and bright,
While thunder claps, but not in fright.
Clouds wear hats, all fluffy and round,
In this carnival, joy is found.

So raise a toast with a goofy grin,
To moments where the fun can begin.
In this vibrant veil, life's a game,
Laughs and giggles are the name.

Skylines Full of Stories

Buildings twist like pretzel rolls,
Chimneys puffing silly moles.
Windows wink with cheeky glee,
Sharing secrets, one, two, three.

A crow wears glasses, reads the news,
While squirrels shuffle in their shoes.
Tales of neighbors, wild and bright,
Performers under the starry night.

Balloons float high, plotting pranks,
While passersby give quizzical thanks.
Every rooftop has its say,
In this lively, funny ballet.

So look up high, let your heart roam,
In the skyline's tales, we find our home.
With laughter creeping through each street,
Life's a funny joy to greet.

The Living Tapestry

Threads of laughter weave and sigh,
Swirling colors catch the eye.
Each stitch tells its comical tale,
A fabric where the giggles sail.

There's a hedgehog knitting hats,
While rabbits tap dance with the bats.
Silly patterns, twists and spins,
In this place, the fun begins.

Petunias sing in off-key tune,
While daisies teach the bees to swoon.
Every thread a memory spun,
Crafting moments full of fun.

So let's weave joy with every sigh,
In this tapestry, we'll fly high.
With laughter stitched and hearts so free,
Life's a colorful mystery.

The Everchanging Scene

Birds in bow ties dance with glee,
Squirrels in shades sip iced tea.
A dog in a tutu, twirls with flair,
A cat on a ladder—what a sight to wear!

A ladybug wearing a tiny hat,
Jumps on a sunflower, oh look at that!
A butterfly joins the funky beat,
While ants in a line march on their feet.

Frogs jump high, trying to compete,
With a snail who glides, oh-so discreet.
Each moment's a joke in this vibrant scene,
Nature's a circus, you know what I mean!

Umbrellas of petals sway with the breeze,
As goofy raccoons rummage with ease.
In this lively panorama we find,
Laughter and cheer, oh so unconfined!

The Sprightly Frame

The sun peeks in with a cheeky grin,
While flowers giggle, where do we begin?
A parrot quips with a playful squawk,
As bunnies bounce like they're on a walk!

A squirrel climbs up with a nutty plan,
While kittens prance, quite like they can.
The trees sway along, a wiggly dance,
In this bustling world, everything has a chance!

In corner chairs, ladybugs chat,
About the latest cat fashion—imagine that!
A hedgehog stumbles, but never feels sad,
For all of his pals are there to be glad!

A drinking straw hat fits just right,
On a merry old turtle, ready for flight.
With laughter wrapped in colors bright,
Life chuckles on, morning till night!

Nature's Wagging Tail

The grass giggles as the wind does play,
While daisies shout, 'What a lovely day!'
A dog rolls over, splashing in dirt,
Then shakes it all off, 'Oh, what a spurt!'

A hedgehog zooms by on a trike,
Shouting, 'Watch out!' as he takes a hike.
Butterflies join in, flapping with style,
Making us chuckle, what a great while!

A fish on a skateboard flips with glee,
While frogs applaud, 'How cool can you be?'
The sun beams down, a spotlight above,
In this lively stage, we're all full of love!

The trees gently giggle, swaying along,
With roots tapping softly to a quirky song.
Life's a romp in this playful tale,
Where joy has a tail that will never fail!

The Colorful Mosaic

In hues of laughter, the flowers bloom,
A rainbow of giggles erupts in the room.
Bees wearing shoes buzz round the way,
While clouds shaped like kittens brighten the day!

The breeze tosses colors, a painter's delight,
With shades of silliness dancing in sight.
A frog in polka dots hops with a cheer,
While all of creation leans in to hear!

A jolly old owl throws a party at night,
With fireflies twinkling, oh what a sight!
Balloons made of petals float up high,
As whiskered raccoons munch on pie!

Within this mosaic, every face glows,
With nature's own humor spilling in rows.
In colors of fun, life's tapestry sways,
Each moment a brushstroke of whimsical ways!

Through the Shimmering Glass

Through the glass, a dog goes by,
Chasing birds, oh my, oh my!
He leaps and bounds, a furry sprite,
Then trips and falls, what a silly sight!

A cat observes with narrowed eyes,
From her perch, she quietly spies.
The dog's antics bring her glee,
She chuckles softly, oh, the irony!

Plants wave gently in the breeze,
Dancing like they're on their knees.
A pot drops down, what a scare!
Debris and dirt fly everywhere!

Sunshine brightens this hilarious scene,
With laughter painted in shades of green.
Nature's a circus, oh can't you see?
Behind every glass, there's comedy!

Sunlit Daydreams

In the sun, a squirrel performs,
Gathering nuts, oh how he storms!
He drops one, oops, look at him go,
That nut's rolled away, up the road, oh no!

Butterflies flutter, in quest for treats,
While ants march forward in disciplined beats.
A sunflower grins, it's such a show,
It sways to the tunes of nature's flow.

A breezy gust disrupts the fun,
Knocking hats off, oh my, just run!
With giggles echoing through the air,
Each face turns round, what a funny scare!

Bubbles float by, they shimmer bright,
Catch them quickly, what a delight!
But just as you reach, they pop with a sigh,
And we laugh at how dreams can just fly by!

The Natural Reverie

Down by the pond, a frog leaps high,
In search of flies, oh my, oh my!
He misses one, splashes around,
But with a splash, he's glory bound!

A turtle lumbers, it's fashionably late,
Sporting a shell, isn't that great?
He peeks at the frog, gives a slow wink,
While the pond's ripples make everyone think!

A dragonfly zooms, it's so fancy and fast,
Suddenly stops, oh, what a blast!
The frog and turtle break into cheer,
As a picnic unfolds, oh how they steer!

Nature chuckles at her own silly art,
With each twist of fate that plays a part.
In this wild theatre, we find much to see,
With quirky antics of creatures, oh me!

Voices of the Breeze

Whispers of wind play with the leaves,
Tickling branches, oh what a tease!
A spirited gust sends a hat in flight,
Chasing it down, oh what a sight!

A rabbit hops, with flair and pride,
Dreaming of carrots, his favorite ride.
But as he prances, and stops to munch,
He leaps in fright at a buzzing crunch!

The bees hum a tune, their work never done,
Sweet honey dreams, it's all in the fun!
They bump and zoom, in joyful disarray,
A slapstick ballet, oh what a play!

Clouds drift by, actors in the sky,
Changing the scene with a fluffy sigh.
As laughter rises from the ground below,
Nature's humor is ready to show!

Frames of Wonder

In frames of wood, a show bizarre,
A cat in boots and a dancing star.
The goldfish grips his microphone,
Singing tunes in a fishy tone.

When squirrels parade in tiny hats,
And umbrellas bloom where the window's at.
The world outside spins tales so bright,
In the laughter of day and the chatter of night.

Bunnies hop on the stretch of grass,
While a snail hops by, moving quite fast.
With painted skies and giggling trees,
This scene of joy is sure to please.

Oh, how the world can twist and twirl,
With cupcakes flying and dogs that swirl!
In this frame, let your worries dissipate,
As life outside throws a marvelous fate.

The Hidden Mosaic

Peeking out, what do I see?
A bird on the roof, sipping tea!
The neighbor's cat juggles three mice,
All while wearing a sweater quite nice.

A tortoise teaching yoga poses,
To bushes full of wombat roses.
The sun sneezes, spreads rays of cheer,
As clouds giggle, "I'm over here!"

A kite with googly eyes takes flight,
Dancing with laughter, oh what a sight!
In a world of color, let spirits climb,
Where every moment feels like prime time.

Here in the chaos of painted views,
Rain boots parade in polka-dot shoes.
It's all a riddle, a puzzling game,
Where the odd is ordinary and the same is insane.

Fluttering Leaves and Bright Skies

Leaves gossip like old friends do,
When butterflies play peek-a-boo.
The clouds wear socks of rainbow hues,
While frogs debate the best of blues.

The sun beams down, wearing a grin,
As squirrels prepare for a nutty spin.
With acorns bouncing on the ground,
And bees buzzing silly all around.

A parade of ants in marching line,
While mushrooms gather for a wine and dine.
The daisies laugh, their heads held high,
As a sneaky snail crawls by, oh my!

The air is filled with jolly sound,
As nature's circus spins around.
With every flutter, a burst of cheer,
In this lively play, the fun is near!

The Alive Horizon

Beyond the edge, where silliness reigns,
The cows wear shades while dancing on trains.
While pigs in capes fly up with glee,
In a world made of jelly and green tea.

The horizon stretches, a canvas so wide,
With paintbrush trees growing side by side.
Kites made of cookies soar in the breeze,
While the wind tickles as it pleases.

An octopus juggles while dressed in flair,
And whispers secrets of flying underwear.
Every ray becomes a wink and a sigh,
Inviting you to join the quirky high.

So peek outside, don't be shy,
Catch laughter as it zooms by.
In this alive and whimsical scene,
Life spins around like a well-oiled machine!

www.ingramcontent.com/pod-product-compliance
Lightning Source LLC
Chambersburg PA
CBHW050305120526
44590CB00016B/2492